SandCastle 2

What Do You See?

In a Valley

Mary Elizabeth Salzmann

ABDO
Publishing Company

Published by SandCastle™, an imprint of ABDO Publishing Company, 4940 Viking Drive, Edina, Minnesota 55435.

Printed in the United States.

Cover and interior photo credits: Corbis Images, Corel, PhotoDisc.

Library of Congress Cataloging-in-Publication Data

Salzmann, Mary Elizabeth, 1968-
In a valley / Mary Elizabeth Salzmann.
p. cm -- (What do you see?)
ISBN 1-57765-569-9
1. Valleys--Juvenile literature. [1. Valleys.] I. Title.
QH87.2 .S25 2001
578.7--dc21 2001022012

The SandCastle concept, content, and reading method have been reviewed and approved by a national advisory board including literacy specialists, librarians, elementary school teachers, early childhood education professionals, and parents.

Let Us Know

After reading the book, SandCastle would like you to tell us your stories about reading. What is your favorite page? Was there something hard that you needed help with? Share the ups and downs of learning to read. We want to hear from you! To get posted on the Abdo Publishing Company Web site, send us email at:

sandcastle@abdopub.com

About SandCastle™

Nonfiction books for the beginning reader

- Basic concepts of phonics are incorporated with integrated language methods of reading instruction. Most words are short, and phrases, letter sounds, and word sounds are repeated.
- Readability is determined by the number of words in each sentence, the number of characters in each word, and word lists based on curriculum frameworks.
- Full-color photography reinforces word meanings and concepts.
- "Words I Can Read" list at the end of each book teaches basic elements of grammar, helps the reader recognize the words in the text, and builds vocabulary.
- Reading levels are indicated by the number of flags on the castle.

Look for more SandCastle books in these three reading levels:

Level 1
(one flag)

Grades Pre-K to K
5 or fewer words per page

Level 2
(two flags)

Grades K to 1
5 to 10 words per page

Level 3
(three flags)

Grades 1 to 2
10 to 15 words per page

This is a valley.

Valleys are low areas between hills.

Many valleys have rivers running through them.

Some valleys have gentle slopes.

Other valleys are at the bottom of steep cliffs.

Some **valleys** are deserts.

They have few plants.

Other valleys are covered with trees and grass.

Sheep graze in this valley.

This otter lives in a valley by a river.

What do you see in this valley?

(flowers)

Words I Can Read

Nouns

A noun is a person, place, or thing

bottom (BOT-uhm) p. 11
grass (GRASS) p. 15
otter (OT-ur) p. 19
river (RIV-ur) p. 19
valley (VAL-ee) pp. 5, 17, 19, 21

Plural Nouns

A plural noun is more than one person, place, or thing

areas (AIR-ee-uhz) p. 5
cliffs (KLIFSS) p. 11
deserts (DEZ-urtss) p. 13
flowers (FLOU-urz) p. 21
hills (hilz) p. 5
plants (PLANTSS) p. 13
rivers (RIV-urz) p. 7
sheep (SHEEP) p. 17
slopes (SLOHPSS) p. 9
trees (TREEZ) p. 15
valleys (VAL-eez) pp. 5, 7, 9, 11, 13, 15

Verbs

A verb is an action or being word

are (AR) pp. 5, 11, 13, 15
covered (KUHV-urd) p. 15
do (DOO) p. 21
graze (GRAYZ) p. 17
have (HAV) pp. 7, 9, 13
is (IZ) p. 5
lives (LIVZ) p. 19
running (RUHN-ing) p. 7
see (SEE) p. 21

Adjectives

An adjective describes something

few (FYOO) p. 13
gentle (JEN-tuhl) p. 9
low (LOH) p. 5
many (MEN-ee) p. 7
other (UHTH-ur) pp. 11, 15
some (SUHM) pp. 9, 13
steep (STEEP) p. 11
this (THISS) pp. 17, 19, 21

What Do You See in a Valley?

Match the Words to the Pictures

flowers

river

sheep

tree